Reliquaries

poems by

Liz Kicak

Finishing Line Press
Georgetown, Kentucky

Reliquaries

For my family—my biological, my chosen, and those at the wonderous intersection of both: my deepest love and gratitude.

Copyright © 2025 by Liz Kicak
ISBN 979-8-89990-167-6 First Edition
All rights reserved under International and Pan-American Copyright Conventions. No part of this book may be reproduced in any manner whatsoever without written permission from the publisher, except in the case of brief quotations embodied in critical articles and reviews.

ACKNOWLEDGMENTS

With sincere thanks to the following journals who published previous versions of the following poems, sometimes under different titles.

"Atropos" *Barely South Review* 2011
"Chuck-Will's-Widow", "I Knew God Existed Because", "Reliquaries" *Lincoln Review* 2025
"Girl Eaten by a Tree" *Jersey Devil Press* 2013
"My Mother's Request After an Unannounced Visit" *WomenArts Quarterly* 2012
"Operculum" *Orion* 2018
"Panic Attack at 2:17p.m." *New York Quarterly* 2010
"Sky Takes" *SweetLit* 2018
"Upon Declaring a Poem Unsalvageable" *Tulane Review* 2011

Publisher: Leah Huete de Maines
Editor: Christen Kincaid
Cover Art: *At Night in the Greenhouse 6* by Janaina Tschäpe
Author Photo: Corey Lapak
Cover Design: Elizabeth Maines McCleavy

Order online: www.finishinglinepress.com
       also available on amazon.com

Author inquiries and mail orders:
Finishing Line Press
PO Box 1626
Georgetown, Kentucky 40324
USA

Contents

Index 1
In the Beginning 2
Recipe for the Devourable 3
Reliquaries 4
Spellbound 5
Sky Takes 6
Genealogy 7
Poet Visits the Ophthalmologist 8
The Island of Stability 9
Not a Mask, but a Head 10
Curriculum 11
On Contemplating Celibacy 12
Genesis 13
Outside Destiny, Florida 15
Apocalypse: Prophecy 16
I Knew God Existed Because 17
Panic Attack at 2:17p.m. 18
My Mother's Request After an Unannounced Visit 19
Common Wildflowers 20
Apocalypse: Dream 21
Upon Declaring a Poem Unsalvageable 22
Operculum 23
A Rare and Glorious Thing 24
The Inevitability of Blooming 25
Sinkhole 26
Belly Dancing for Beginners 27
A Certain Kind of Grief 28
Girl Eaten By a Tree 29

- Atropos 30
- Chuck-Will's Widow 31
- Anosmia 32
- Fieldwork 33
- Walking with the Orbweaver 34
- Trespassing 36
- First Wave 37
- Butcher Bunny 38
- I Will Make Your House a Rookery 40
- Dispatches from the Still Life 42
- Drawers Full of Ulnas 43
- Sink or Swim 44
- Hollandse Nieuwe 45
- Florida Haibun with Cat 46
- The Throats of Our Wrists Brave Lilies 47
- Another Pale Thing 48

This tease of rain and adventure, this swarm
Of impatient daisies, this beating heart,
For so may I be forever infested with angels.
—*Jay Hopler*

Index

Never have I finished a whole book
without thumbing to the last pages:
Who dunnit? Who survives? Don't let me

attach my heart to unseen breakers—
I'm weary from the unexpected
slayings of main characters I love

by other main characters I love.
But this is pageless. We are pageless.
My words unordered. Have I never

dunnit? Who survives who? Let me don't—
dearest, let me don't run to ruin
the ending with fear and weariness.

Never have I softened in a palm
or rolled my eyes in perfect sync like
I soften and roll with you, your palm,

your rolling eyes. Dearest, I worry
what I might do to your heart, or worse
I'll bore it to stupor and certain

death. Never have I been anyone's
main character—be not a plot twist,
or worse, the unexpected slayer.

Through me thumb and annotate my palms,
my rolling eyes. My sabotage, run
to ruin it, dear. Run. Ruin it.

Sync our survival, finish me whole.
Are there words for this? Unordered words:
pageless ruin. Roll softly, love. Run.

In the Beginning

The chipped St. Francis statue watches
from his shelf above the kitchen sink
while the girl's father baits traps.
Mice are so small, snow so deep—
surely they could spare space
behind the dryer, an attic corner.
Plus, killing is a sin.
*Not this kind. Jesus doesn't want
diseased mice in our house,* he says,
baiting the gap between stove and wall.

By morning, every trap is clean.
This is the beginning of her education
in fatherhood's invisible work:
hiding slaughter, lying to his daughter
who kept vigil for the death snap.
It must have been the first time
she felt that invisible
vice around her neck—that crush
that still haunts her throat when the house creaks
or men speak of God.

Recipe for the Devourable

How glassy are the eyes?
Blot the body. Gently
towel it down. Blade rock,
head sever—it will be easier
if she can't stare back.

Hook the gills, pull
spine through skin.
Fiberglass bones, exotic
perfume of a far-off sea.

Blade slips between skin
and muscle. Scales like
a sequined skirt
pooled beside a bed.

Cleaved. Pink, glistening
in open air. Blot the body
gently. Towel it down.
Feel the frail resistance
of meat without bones—how
it submits without its spine.

Reliquaries

Glittered forgeries,
cayenne-tongued and bursting
with skull-howl
hornetswarm, lemon juice
in cat scratches and fingernails
clutching open air. Sprint,

lungs full of salt, veins full of voices.
Sing. Hot skin snapping, suffocated
by bodies. Alone.
Bless all corners like rice
spilled on tile floors. Lure the ghosts—
mandibles of sinners and saints.

What are words if not the gilded homes
of timeworn bones and teeth?

Spellbound

That idiot forgot his magic words again.
Mothers rush to cover their children's eyes,
hide the horror of the empty box. Everyone's
so busy demanding refunds (where's the magic
of turning nothing into nothing?) no one considers
she might be lost, sharing a false bottomed trunk
with frightened doves, suffocating under silk scarves,
white rabbits, ears stuffed with quarters,
mouth full of curses and lockpicks for her handcuffs.
She's done being his vaudeville ornament.
And anyway, the sequins give her hives, smiling
hurts her jaw, and those fucking feather boas
make her sneeze. Fine—she'll take the trick cards,
his black cape, and the one rabbit that doesn't bite.

Sky Takes

The slightest breeze sends me into hysterics. Last year
was the Tornado Summer, sirens common as cicadas.

Ten seconds of fury to shred acres of forest, rubble whole towns.
Grown men weeping beside the wreckage of a life.

That's wrong—it's not the grief that terrified me, but witnessing
a thing openly rage with enough fury to drive people underground,

into halls to huddle under mattresses and pray.
Instead of clutching anger like a stone, the sky desires

so the sky takes. Screaming through orange groves, mangroves,
mailboxes, strip mall, cattle ranch. Such conviction in shrieking

across the land with shameless want, the indulgence of frenzy
and disregard for scarring what it loves.

Genealogy

Great Great Aunt Elizabeth and her husband,
her husband's brother and wife,
and his wife's sister were all struck barren
by the herbicide they sprayed on their corn.

But weeds taught me the art of paying attention.
Perched on a swing or grass-sprawled,
I found every four-leaf clover in my orbit.
It's a thing I still do (not collect shamrocks)
soften my eyes when overwhelmed,
wait for something to sharpen in the blur.

My father surrendered his backyard
to clover each summer—a sacrifice
I wouldn't understand until years later
as he regales me with mole cricket victories
or how he replaces sprinkler heads:
Like a pit crew changing tires mid-race.
Which makes as much sense to me as my father
comparing himself to a jackrabbit or a tennis racket.
He gave me books to press my daily harvest:
four-leaf clovers staining hundreds of pages.

When the doctor says my childbearing
window is closing I remember Elizabeth,
her corn fields. What if they'd surrendered
to horseweed and foxtail? Yes, even to clover?
There are worse outcomes—
the field of our ancestry fertile with proof.

A brittle shamrock I lodged in the spine
of my father's book falls to rest on his knee.
As lucky as anything I could give him these days.
Sprinklers hiss across his pristine lawn.

Poet Visits the Ophthalmologist

He's embarrassed—like he walked in
while I was dressing instead
of mumbling *sclera* over and over
(litanies a favorite nervous tool).

I tell him sclera is a lovely word,
the best option from the eyeball
diagram on his wall—all those
consonants competing for the tongue.

His throat clear and white coat
straightening suggest he's never tasted
words before. This fixer who dyes my eye
electric yellow and makes the scar tissue glow.

He will scoop it out with his tiny surgical
melon-baller (You just winced didn't you?
Don't worry. It did not make the wet sucking sound
of gouging a ripe melon).

Like a miner on a dig, a light strapped
to his head, melon-baller in one hand,
lens in the other, he leans in close, so close
his knee brushes my thigh.

I can see fine gray hairs at his temple,
the shading around his parted lips,
how his tongue presses his top teeth
in deep concentration and I remember

the first time I let a boy see me naked
I was just like this: skittish, resisting
the urge to bolt. I think sclera and don't blink.
The doctor's breath on my cheek.

The Island of Stability

The first time I said I loved you
I'd never felt so heavy—
microscopic
yet impossibly dense
heavier than lead
the element of touch-poison
mouth-poison.
We paint our walls
ignore the symptoms
of our sickening.

The heaviest elements
are man-made
highly unstable.
Atoms slam together
spawn a new element.
It lives a microsecond
or two before dying
of spontaneous fission
triggering that predictable
half-life.

Scientists dream
of a fission-less sweet spot
where elements live for years:
The Island of Stability—
strictly theoretical of course
stability always is
and some things shouldn't
be fused no matter how
fascinating their decay chain.

Not a Mask, but a Head
>After the painting *Melpomene, The Muse of Tragedy,*
>by Elisabetta Sirani

Here they come. Again.
Men flocking to my altar
with their offerings
of vintage typewriters,
alcoholism, and goddess fetishes.
I can't believe I put my book down for this.

Stop saying *tragedy*,
you mean tedious:
leaving a naked woman in bed to cry,
you light your cigarette in the rain
under a flickering streetlight
six blocks from home
and your other crying woman.
Sex and tears are easy—
go to my sisters for that shit.

You know what's hard? Silence.
A cut so deep it severs vocal chords.
Give me a hunk of Grecian flesh
to gnaw, spit out, let it wander
the mountain forever mute.
Zeus did give me a sword after all,
but not a mask—painters got that wrong.

On my altar leave
not a mask, but a head
and for my bookmark, a tongue.

Curriculum

My nephew grabs cereal in his grimy hand to feed me
through video. I crunch and smack my lips but his fist
remains full. He smashes his breakfast to my pixilated mouth,
fails again, realizes I'm lying—realizes lying exists.
Then tears and a crack of fury.

But it's not the rage I'm used to seeing in men's eyes,
rage like lightning—sudden and catastrophic.
The tricks women master to avoid being struck,
hoarding umbrellas in case storm clouds threaten.
It's a lesson we learn early. I picked up my sister
from a high school party once. I don't have to
ask. Rain hits like it hates our windshield.

No. When my nephew slaps the screen, my stomach
twists with guilt. I reach for my keys to speed across town,
lick soggy oats from his fingers, when he calls my name,
kisses the screen, leaving magnified flecks of spit
my sister wipes clean with the back of her hand. *I'm sorry*, I say.
She laughs, asks why I'm apologizing for her son's tantrum.
No, I say. *Not for that.*

On Contemplating Celibacy

> *The Ghost Orchid grows in deep swamps—an endangered species that should not be removed from the wild.*
> —*Florida's Native Orchids*

She will miss the heart leap
of the hunt, the double back,
slack jawed wonder that turns
miles of muck-trek to nothing
and the perfume of dirt under nails,
brush of swamp steeped thigh,
the stubbled face's whisper of breath.
But not the stem snap. Never the stem snap,
slow death in an urn. Pining to be
unpluckable, she rootwraps mangroves,
knits herself into wild cypress.

Genesis

Amoeba: Litter of overtures

Blackberry: Tart droplets in spike swam

Catfish: Slippery whiskered silt sieve

Desert: Heat sea, shelter from green

Elephant: Devoted mountain slow to anger

Flamingo: Grinning pink puddle wader

Gardenia: Calm breath. White star rising in jade field

Heart: Gift

Island: Dizzy planets in lapping orbits

Jellyfish: Water cloud with bite

Kingfisher: Cobalt in flight with sunrise'd stomach

Lips: Doorways

Mosquito: Needled blood-sipper. Plague darling

Nectarine: Giddy tree ornamented with crip, hissing joy

Ocean: Approximate heaven

Palm: Storm-limber branch whip

Quillfish: Shiny moon-charmed silver sliver

Retina: Meadows of gloves awaiting hands

Snow: Devotion

Tiger: Hunger-lust. Teeth snapping, loyal muscle

Unicorn: Recalled

Vanilla: Pellets of warm wood and cream

Waterfall: Liquid altar. Nexus of cascading angel wings

Xiaosaurus: Beloved bone mystery

Yarrow: Ceaseless lace on stems

Zebra: Painted night with cracks and hooves

Outside Destiny, Florida

What could the grazing cattle be eating?
Nothing but roadside spikey scrub brush.

Fire lines hoed into the ground.
Burned grass, parched skeletons of leafless trees.

A billboard reminds me a baby's heart beats
eighteen days after conception.

In Nebraska, these might be fields of ripened wheat
but here, just miles of death gone to seed.

An old tire, tethered to a fence,
with "Jesus Saves" painted around the rim.

Surely the cows are starving.

Apocalypse: Prophesy

I hope the plane crashes. My empty seat
bound for a reunion with friends
I could not face. Premonition the more romantic excuse.

It would be a beautiful day for it though—cloudless sky, a touch of fall.

Acorns plummet from oak branches,
patter down my roof, thunk in the yard—
my world of small omens. I saw myself at cruising altitude,

unlatching the escape panel over the wing, being sucked into blue sky.
        Cloudless. A touch of fall.

Do bodies falling from planes hit the earth?
        Breadcrumbing cornfields to the crash site?

Movies only show the hero in a nylon halo, but even villains have to land
        somewhere—smash through a suburban roof, plunk into a duck
        pond,
                impale on the tallest pine in a forest of tall pines.

Don't they?
Or would the wind and weight of sky shear the body, atomizing it into the only cloud?

I Knew God Existed Because

my hands shook the entire time.
Always had a faith-craving
heart and he was an answered prayer with skin
steeped in rain and song, skin that stung the wasp.
I believed when he spoke—said I was the moth
that draws the flame, the spell that casts the witch.

He spoke and I believed
until song became our second skin. Dizzy,
breathless—like breathing in a closed garage
with the car running. Laughter in the face
of all that poison, until we spilled into the night
where the moon on his skin was holy and I believed

in the sanctity of that moment. Wasn't it fun
when I became the rain-singing girl? Your girl
with flung-wide windows in a raging storm.
Wasn't I biblical in my blind faith for our world
predestined to flood?

Panic Attack at 2:17p.m.

Cockroaches.
Cockroaches scurry
under my skin.
Thousands of legs
antennae tremble
twitch scuttle
in my stomach
swarm ears
rush down legs
scratch until I bleed.
Mouth of copper dust
tongue-coated
raisining the lungs.
Throat choke
adrenaline gag.
Heart pulsing grenade
pin pulled.
Blood sears veins
melts skin
lays bare cheekbones
eye sockets. Smolder—
even the bugs are panicking.

My Mother's Request After an Unannounced Visit

Will you call me in the morning? Her voice
fear-streaked in a way I hadn't heard since I was five,
said the berries from the front yard tree were sour.

A soapy plate clatters to the floor,
she plunges a finger down my throat
until I gag into her open hands.

A soothsayer reading her daughter's fortune,
sifting through her slop-slicked hands.
Three empty red sacs—shed skins of holly berries.

Oh, Thank God. She rinses her hands, collapses
against the counter for days before remembering
I was there, bile-stung throat, petrified

of the animal she'd become. The animal
that made me retch, shrieked at my father
to hack the tree down before dinner.

Warrior mother armed with shovel and spade,
ousting stump, chopping roots, salting earth.
I recoil from this rabid assassin.

They're poisonous, baby. Trembling hands
on either side of my face and that tone
I wouldn't hear for another twenty-three years:

I would die if I lost you.

Common Wildflowers
a Found Poem

Touch-me-not bloodroot.
Toothy doll's eyes hooded,
hidden, capable of holding
milk-sickness. Notched,
nodding uvula.

Masses of blooming cutleaf
toothwort, snakeroot. Finely
dissected nectar guides,
a necessary food—fruit, a blue-
black berry.

Umbrella vaguely resembles teeth
like all milkweeds, plume-like,
heart-leaved, grown ornamentally.
Whorl of three ripe seed capsules
showy, toxic. Uncommon
treasures, suggestive shades
of violet petals floodplain
from dusk to dawn.

Bindweed, favorite
of the hummingbirds
supposedly died
from leaf litter. Spike of
showy white canopy gaps,
touch-me-not ripe seed.

Apocalypse: Dream

Every night, algae-tipped
propellers chop a glass sea,
I thu-thump under the bow.

Water rushes my throat
blades smack my teeth—
playing cards in bike spokes.

Next comes the fish mob, ravenous
for vitreous, gums, veins. The joy
of my body being useful for once.

I had an aquarium as a girl, obsessed
over a swarm of flashing tetras
when food flakes bled over the water.

I still love a good cloud of scales and fins.

Upon Declaring a Poem Unsalvageable

What if they *are* like eggs?

A predetermined pile stitched inside before my birth.

Scarce though they are, I have abandoned one—
        words made by   made of my body,
              I have surrendered one to the abyss

declared her irredeemable
        primordially flawed, destined to shrivel,

        to rot on the vine
        like fruit unharvested.

Operculum

Lord, make me Lazarus
and raise me from the silt
before I fossilize in the mouth
of the rill. At least make me a fish,
sprout gills so I may breathe.
Cleave my sides and I will bleed
into half-moons until this newly ruffled neck
nectars air from water.

If not a fish, just pleats fluttering in the spate.
Neither fin, nor tail—but let me live forever
submerged in this river of the unsayable,
a cleric always searching for the word for
glint on water when sun passes through a lattice of trees
as cormorant breaks the surface, bobbing and breathing.

A Rare and Glorious Thing
> After the painting *Breakfast of the Birds*, Gabriele Münter

Crack of yellow on white branch,
blue gash of sky, skeletal trees
freeze mid-reach in the bitter morning
where kestrels shiver in hallows,
cats search out fireplaces and barns,
and though frost-nipped on their wingtips
cardinals and goldfinches sing
the full-throated verse of the unhunted.
Nests empty, bellies full of winter
berries, all enemies asleep.
And isn't it a rare and glorious thing
to be safe enough to drop into the belly,
toss the head back, pierce the morning with song?
But there is a woman through the curtains
who refuses to stir sugar into her coffee
for fear of the spoon's clink. Mutely perched
on her chair, a nest of hair curled, pinned
to the back of her brittle neck.
She closes her eyes, imagines notes
bursting past her teeth, shattering the window,
plunging the house into feather and rime.

The Inevitability of Blooming

If I were a tulip, I would be nervous
hoping for resurrection, but I've never had
my mother's faith in dirt and revival.

They look dead long before she condemns them
to burial under feet of freeze. Like onions
forgotten in the pantry—rock hard, black.

I've never had my mother's faith in anything,
certainly not the inevitability of blooming:
quickening roots, sun-straining stems.

Even though I've seen her raise gardens
during blizzards with nothing but a nail,
sugar, drops of color named Desert Plum,

Pearl Dust. English roses bloom from the tip
of an icing bag, the nail revolves slowly, she sprouts
layers of petals, greenhouses the kitchen,

gives us peonies, chrysanthemums. The counter
fields of lavender. Lily of the valley, lilacs plume
from the table, morning glory and hydrangea

spill from the kitchen. Everything outdoors
can wither and rot. We will never go without
sugared violets and tulips—especially tulips.

Sinkhole
> *And the earth opened its mouth and swallowed them up, with their households and all the people who belonged to Korah and all their goods.*
> —Numbers 16:32

It's a gamble: living
on cleave-hungry earth
with our lust and our rage
and our false idols.

Across town, a man's house
was swallowed while he slept.
Wreathes rim the pit's perimeter
but it refuses to give up the body.

And we are all Korahites here,
living on leased plague
and borrowed time.
Earth's appetite is insatiable,

anointed, cleansing like fire
but without smoke, or ash,
or spark of warning.
Just massive self-collapse,

a sudden unannounced burial,
convocation in the belly of the earth.

Belly Dancing for Beginners

She wants to say jiggle,
pointing to her torso's fluid flicks
but knows better than to speak fat
words. Knows we seek to silence flesh-
slap, muzzle thigh and gut.

Except it does jiggle—this vessel
for the hip's exhale jiggles
when she shimmies. Thighs hum,
belly catches the tune. Wrist roll,
shoulder shake into boneless wave.

The body sings louder, louder
until fat is overwhelmed into joyful noise,
swirls like dervishes. A breathing hymn,
a chorus of quiver and quake, she is all
whirl and chant, jiggle and praise.

A Certain Kind of Grief
>After a dress in the *2016 Spring/Summer Collection*, Rodarte

A docent asks for my favorite in a gallery of forms
draped in silks, chiffon mille feuille, hemmed in crystals.
The head-to-toe organza mourning gown. Obviously.

Hand stitched requiem: capelet, cravat buttoned to the throat,
vertical ruffles to the ankle. A woman's somber cocoon, dignified
but for its rabid yellow hue, a raging lemon cloud.

Monochromatic graveside hysteria—the scandal this dress will incite
in those who've never known the spastic energy of grief,
of misery so electric it crackles under the skin.

When she leans down to place a rose on the casket lid,
this dress embraces the vulagarity of loss, allows
the briefest glimpse of widow navel.

Girl Eaten by a Tree
      After the painting by the same name by Mark Ryden

Her two remaining friends stagger
back. Mute. Carry her shoes
like the flag of a fallen soldier.
They'd been skipping among
larkspur, pines, clover, gossip,
chittering chipmunks, never suspecting
that innocuous alcove in the oak
where robins fought to lay their eggs
would soon be stuffed with one of them.

He's devastated but starving,
rooted in place. Branches wrap her
slight waist, he shovels her in
headfirst, feels her screams in his gut.
She kicks, flails, his throat churns
with gold ringlets until he gags,
nearly spits her out, but now
he's got the taste for candied flesh.

So sweet! Like peach nectar.
Bark breaks the body—the joy
of feasting. Shoulders, still
in a blue frock, slip down.
Peal buttons slide over his tongue.
The slight puff of her belly, syrupy
hips and thighs—thighs soaked
in maple sap, marinated in treacle.
Even her socks are sugared.

Atropos

I see the bird's body first—neck cocked
at an angle only the dead can bear.
The same daily route, dog tethered to my wrist.
He tugs me away from the wren in the gutter.

        "Pneumonia," a voice echoes.
        He is a hot air balloon
        roped off and tied to a riddled body,
        leashed to a bed with tubes and wires.

She is bloated and sour the next morning.
Ants absconded with her eyes in the night.
Hundreds funnel through her beak eating
their way through throat and lung.

        My hands are feathered—sleek, black.
        I wake to the phantom smell of bleach,
        tragically earthbound, stomach fluttering
        at something just forgotten.

Florida is cruel to the dead. Damp heat
arousing maggot and roach.
A picked-clean carcass—
even her claws poached by bugs.

        How did I become the severing sister?
        A final breathless glance
        at gray temples, yellowed skin.
        Excarnation as a rush of wings.

The last bone and feather gone.
Pneuma and corpse unknotted.
A stain on the cement, her tombstone.
Tomorrow's rain will wash it away.

        Everyone has them—
        dreams of plummeting.
        Jolting awake, panting,
        alone, drowning in dark.

Chuck-Will's Widow

Throlling, looping cries wake me
every night. Audio clips by the dozen:
Killdeer. Bobwhite. Willet.
Wrong bird. Wrong Bird. Wrong Bird.
I finally find her in an almanac:
Chuck-Will's Widow. I email my Papa—
he knows the victory of naming,
the taxonomy of heartbeats. He taught me
warblers: blue-winged, prairie, yellow-throated,
but never a widow bird.

Yet, I've forgotten (how do I keep forgetting?)
he is ash in an unseen urn
nested in the back of my grandparent's closet.
His shirts still hung and ordered
first by season, then by color.
Grams takes him out and cries at night
when she thinks no one can hear.
There is no database, no register
naming this sound that tears across the glade.

Anosmia

I want to plunge my head into the oak table
where Papa stored his pipe tobacco.
Draw the tang of earth and amber
into my lungs, manifesting their living
room: shale mantle, ivory drapes, his recliner,
this little table stacked with books and briar pipe.

He tamps leaf into the chamber,
shakes a matchbox twice, goes to the porch.
That scent survives in his clothes, his hair.
For months, Grams refused to wash their sheets.
Soap and time stealing his smell until this table
with its tobacco-infused drawer, is the last reserve
and even that is fading.

Fading. Slowly but enough to make me
want to smack her arthritic hand
when she opens the drawer, lets some of him escape.
I need to sieve the air, stockpile his tiny pieces
like when he died—that last alive breath,
Papa atoms drifting like smoke.
Me, useless, watching them go.

Fieldwork
>After *Insects of Surinam, Plate 11* by Maria Sibylla Merian

You cannot know the silk moth until you've seen her
birth a grapevine of eggs along the vein of a palisade leaf.
How pheromones call blind larvae together,
weaving a sweater of second bark.

Hike the jungle in torch light and sweat,
mosquitos plunging at every swath of pungent skin.
Crouch in weeds until the bodies stir,
strike out to strip leaves until sunrise.

Admire the shock of finding a nest of corpses,
trogon hatchlings, mouths still full of larval mush.
Such poison in this land of venoms! That shock
at the back of your sunburned neck is critical to know

the silk moth. Watch worms grow drowsy, the rusting
of their gold bands before shedding, and smell the sweet
rot of discarded cocoons as one rests in your palm,
flexing its new wings, your entire hand hidden in its span.

Walking with the Orbweaver

Worn boardwalk planks press the soles
of my feet, draw me down the live oak,
Spanish moss tunnel where I hide when
I need the world to die for a little while.

I haven't talked to my sister in weeks.

So many spiders call this place home.
In the rain, the webs look lit, hammock
between branches. Venomous-looking
spider, spotted white, red-rimmed
spines, perches in the center of a tire-sized
web, egg sack spun on adjacent leaves—
so many waiting babies.

I should call her when I get home.

Rain, rhythmic as a heartbeat. Yellowed
leaves, pink mold lodged in wood slivers,
slickening the boards. I'm in deep enough
it's just me and the water now. I'm dying
to know what kind of spider that is.

I'm dying to know what her doctor said.

Two limpkins pull snails from under a mangrove.
Mangroves look like family—as if ten saplings
fighting for the same piece of shore closed ranks,
made a pact and fused into one another.

She once told me, "Being human is not for sissies."

Vertigo strikes like lighting. I white knuckle
the railing, focus on a still log in the river until
my vision stops swaying. I'm chilled and envious
of the leafy blanket that insulates dark water.
How, when an obstacle obstructs its creeping
the blanket splits apart, sidesteps,
knits itself together on the other side.

She's right and we do not mend as quickly as flora.
A blue heron tosses off the rain, runs a beak
up and under one wing, then the other, balancing
on an algae-quilted branch even though the wind
picks up and the sky threatens worse. I want to
tell her not to bother. I want to tell her
a worse storm is coming.

Two days from now I will know

the spider is called a Spinybacked Orbweaver.

Trespassing

My sisters and I flop into the sea
of floral comforters smelling of Dad's
cigarettes, and furnace dust. We bury our faces,
smother our giggles. The back corner:
home to everything silk and lace and glitter.
We slip small feet into glamorous heels
we never see her wear. Behind her
Sunday dresses is a cardboard treasure chest.
Inside we find baby teeth, photos of men—
some our father, some not. A plaster handprint
none of us remember making,
two unlabeled cassette tapes,
a dirty white t-shirt around a black bible.
She's coming, Rachel whispers. We duck
behind her wedding dress and winter coats,
hold our breath, hide in ivory lace and gray wool.
She opens the door, rustles the clothes and sings
Where have my little girls gone?

First Wave

Sour milk, rancid
eggs rolled into their cells.

Bodies strapped down,
tipped up. Women who

would rather starve
than be ignored.

A metal funnel driven
past lips cracked from

protests, teeth chip
like tiles. Steel forced

to the throat's base,
a mildewed hose snakes

the esophagus.
It was torture—

being so invisible to choose
self-famine, but if they

could elect nothing else,
why not their deaths?

Even those, stolen with milk,
by men who couldn't stomach

blood on their hands.

Butcher Bunny
        After the poem by the same name by Mark Ryden

Bees cluster around the doorway
drawn by the scent of ham hocks

hung from the ceiling, waxy fat
ripples through muscle. Lamp chops

stacked next to sides of beef.
The pink puppy nibbles a steak,

a mouse laps up blood.
The Butcher Bunny cleaves the flank,

merrily hacks through hide, through bone,
cheeks flushed under the watchful eye

of a plastic dashboard Jesus.
Slit pigs drain to her left,

the bone bucket overflows,
stripped ribs clatter to the floor.

"What would you like, Little Lincoln?"
Butcher Bunny asks. "Smoked gouda

with goat sausage? Aged filets
stuffed with scrambled quail egg

and crab apples? Pork ribs
marinated in spicy mango chili?"

Silently, he points to the fat honeybees.
She nets a baker's dozen in her apron,

wraps them in paper, does not wonder
if he'll eat them stewed, smoked,

pickled in the sweet brine of maple,
bay leaves, and peppercorn.

Butcher Bunny picks up her bone saw,
whistles her dismembering song.

The cat mews for more.

I Will Make Your House a Rookery
for Claire

Suppose that a pregnant woman
frightened by a bird
will have a baby with wings.
What better gift for a child
of the marsh?

So I sneak into your mother's house
with cages full of speckled limpkins,
tuck them behind sofa cushions,
hide flocks of killdeer
in the china cabinet—
a wave of wings makes her shout
each time she needs a plate.

Baskets of eggs—willets warming
in the dryer, sapsuckers
nesting in the pockets
of every coat she owns,
her sock drawer twitters
with winter wrens.

The oven, stuffed with spoonbills,
is pink and hysterical,
while catbirds overtake the pantry,
shred every cereal box
in search of dried berries.

I know your scapulae
are feather-hungry—
I promise to frighten your mother
every day until your birth
so you are never landlocked,
always looking skyward.

The chimney, a breathing tower
of grackles. Behind every door,
a swarm of flycatchers,
gnatcatchers, oystercatchers,

black-crowned herons perch
statute-still on shower rods.
I will flood the plumbing
with piping plovers—
she will bathe in fright and wings,

so you may be born into estuary,
a child of tide and song.

Dispatches from the Still Life
After the painting At the Market Stall, *by Louise Moillon*

I have painted vineyards of grapes
until my fingers crack and bleed
wine. Bristled fuzz over orchards of peaches.

My cruelest insomnia cured
by reciting the ratio of cadmium to madder
to cobalt for the hue of late harvest plums.

Not another pomegranate.
Anything but a pomegranate split, seeds spilled
on a wooden table, juice poised on a knife blade.

I crave the indecent ache of clay,
gray and shapeless so I may dig out hip bones,
sculpt calves—glorious calves!
Compose the sinful arch of a knee.

Colorless, but furiously alive our hands
entwined—I etch palm lines with my fingernail,
mold earth into clavicle, smooth up a neck,
press my thumb to hollow the throat.

And who cares if my parlor is filthened
with castoff clay and silt? I've never had
sweat bead on my brow painting a bowl of fruit.

Drawerful of Ulnas

These days, you educate students on sex,
age, height approximations by letting them
finger your trochlear notch, styloid,
olecranon, where bundles of ligaments
once embraced.

How unfair that your best stories
are all of trauma—healed fractures
seams of calcium along the distal edge,
diet deficiencies, deformities, maybe
how you died. Pathology is palmistry
that says nothing of the flesh or blood,
just bones. No sign of the nights

winding against the capitellum to throw
a baseball to your gangly son at sunset—
cicadas, glove snaps echoing across the lawn.

Nothing left to show where you cradled
an ill lover's neck, the proximal rotation
to lift a hand, check her forehead for fever.

And while I'm on the topic of things
long lost, where is the rest of you?
Once classroom lights dim, doors lock,
do you mourn your missing carpals?
Rifle through neatly labeled drawers
trying them on like ill-fitting shoes?

Sink or Swim
>   *For Dean*

The teacher flings the baby into the pool's deep end,
but when you're small enough to barely splash
the surface, every end is deep. Everything is silent

while she waits for his lungs to ache. Waits.
He sinks to the smooth marcite bottom. She waits
for the evolutionary instinct to kick for air.

How much water did Jesus let Peter drink for his own good
before plucking him from the sea while trying to teach him to walk?
Was Peter calm like the baby or did he thrash like a wounded fish?

She raises him up—he sputters, laughs like he knew
the game all along, his faith in the teacher instead of his legs
or arms or lungs. Even Jesus would be proud.

Hollandse Nieuwe
      After the painting, *Still Life of Fish and Cat*, Clara Peeters

Keep your crawlers, your oyster klatch,
those eels oozing from the bowl.
But this herring is mine.
You will only ruin it with pickling.

I probe the landmine of thready bones,
map chilled meat with tongue and claw.
Share the table, but do not clean when I split
the body; let the wood marinate

so later I remember salt and blood,
remember to bite your stale
stupid fingers, to stake my claim—
oh, firm and glossy eyes!

May the table always taste of herring
eyes: like custard. Like vengeance.

Florida Haibun with Cat

It hits all at once: heat-wet-light. Eyes water and slam shut, lids singe under the sun's rage. My makeup slicks, beads down my face. It's like walking into a kiln underwater—even my shins sweat. Is it my imagination, or do the soles of my shoes soften when they hit the sidewalk like ice-cream the moment is slides off the cone? I slip my key into the hot coal of a doorknob and yellow eyes peer out from under wilted azaleas—the stray black cat seeks amnesty in their shade. We hate each other. I hate the shit she purposefully leaves on the sidewalk. She hates, I gather, my existence and though she tenses, it's too hot to run. It's too hot to run her off too—we're both slogging through 7am and still have six months of summer to face.

Everything melts when
it's hot enough long enough
even enemies

The Throats of Our Wrists Brave Lilies
Title from "Stings," by Silvia Plath

How simple to think
it's all about queen-worship
or the rank-and-file
order of the hive.

Perhaps it is the glow of honey,
comb-warm, oozing over toast. How it
settles in the valleys of the bread,
an old woman easing into her bath.

Maybe it's the tongue's slow slide,
stick surviving on the lips,
a haunt of wings and sugar
in the throat.

Or is it the daily exhilaration
of nearly being stung?

Another Pale Thing

Though each flutter
past my ear startles
and the ceiling is
shadow-washed in wings
I won't strike down
another pale thing
throwing its body
at the light.
I can always spot
a bruised thorax,
the hysterics
of seeking refuge.
I glue flashlights
to the walls, quilt
floors in floodlights,
hang paper lanterns,
chandeliers, anything
with a filament.
Bless tungsten and diodes,
halogen and hindwings.
Bless the drowsy shadow
in the lampshade
and the house
where we sleep
with every light on.

Liz Kicak was born in La Grange, Ohio south of Cleveland and moved to Tampa, Florida with her family in 1997. She maintains a deep love for both the Midwest and the Gulf Coast and the radical differences in climates and cultures. She received her MFA from the University of South Florida in 2011 and now serves as director of the university's Humanities Institute.

Liz discovered a love for ekphrastic poems while on a USF Women in Leadership and Philanthropy Fellowship at the National Museum of Women in the Arts in D.C. Her poems have appeared in the *Tulane Review, New York Quarterly, Orion,* the *Lincoln Review*, and other journals. Liz is her happiest when she's spending time with her niece and nephew, sharing a meal with friends, or playing with her dog, Emmett.

www.ingramcontent.com/pod-product-compliance
Lightning Source LLC
Chambersburg PA
CBHW030059170426
43197CB00010B/1595